Advance praise for *My Friend Fear*

"Experiencing this book feels like sitting in a quiet corner with a trusted friend, having a conversation that affirms your faith in yourself and the world. Meera Lee Patel has taken the big, scary concept of fear and crafted a personal yet universal love letter to it, made all the more beautiful by her ethereal yet down-to-earth illustrations."

—Emily McDowell, creator of Emily McDowell Studio and coauthor of *There Is No Good Card for This*

"Meera Lee Patel is the real deal: philosopher, poet, artist, and emotion-driven intellectual. It can be so easy to let your fears rule your life without noticing it, and so hard to figure out how to stop doing it. Incredibly, this simple, beautiful book offers a real remedy. Patel does more than just lay out a problem and a solution; she takes you by the hand and helps you feel your way closer and closer to a life where you can finally breathe freely and experience the world the way you were born to do. When you're done reading this book, somehow the whole world feels so much more exciting and welcoming. I love this book so much it hurts!"

—Heather Havrilesky, "Ask Polly" columnist for *New York* magazine and author of *How to Be a Person in the World*

"You find certain books and certain books find you. Consider this the latter. Meera makes fear that kid you thought was too cool to be your friend, but turned out to be more like you than you could have imagined. *My Friend Fear* is a beautiful, visual journey into your mind and heart with a very gentle and generous narrator."

—Aparna Nancherla, writer, comedian, and actress

"Meera Lee Patel has this ability to take us through some of our deepest and darkest feelings so we emerge on the other end feeling full and at peace. When Meera writes about fear, she does so in a way that feels like a warm hug, a silent nod from a friend, a soft whisper that she's been there too, and a jubilant shout that she's here for you now and always."

—Jonny Sun, author and illustrator, *everyone's a aliebn when ur a aliebn too*

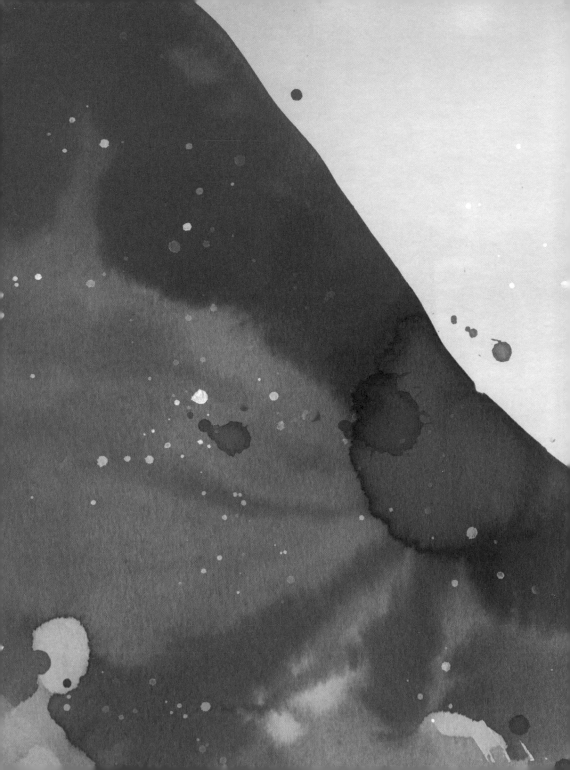

My Friend fear

Finding Magic in the Unknown

MEERA LEE PATEL

A Particular Book

PARTICULAR BOOKS

UK | USA | Canada | Ireland | Australia
India | New Zealand | South Africa

Penguin Books is part of the Penguin Random House group of companies
whose addresses can be found at global.penguinrandomhouse.com.

First published in the United States of America by Tarcher Perigee, an imprint
of Penguin Random House LLC 2018
First published in Great Britain by Particular Books 2018
001

Printed and bound in Italy by L.E.G.O. S.p.A.

A CIP catalogue record for this book is available from the British Library

ISBN: 978–1–846–14974–0

www.greenpenguin.co.uk

MIX
Paper from
responsible sources
FSC® C018179

Penguin Random House is committed to a
sustainable future for our business, our readers
and our planet. This book is made from Forest
Stewardship Council® certified paper.

For my fear,
who stays with me
like moonlight in the darkness
and always leads me
to the magic.

Contents

FEAR
INVITES
THE IMPOSSIBLE
TO HAPPEN.

Author's Note

This is a book about fear. It's a book about longing and loneliness and the way we hide from the world. It's a book about how we hide from ourselves, reluctant to look inside, frightened by what we may find.

This is a book about unlikely friendships, and how to forge the truest relationship you'll ever have the chance to build: the one that connects your heart to your body and mind. You will spend your entire life nurturing this relationship, and there is no better way to spend your time.

This is a book about you, and it's also a book about me. This book is a window that allows us to see each other.

It's a book that stayed in my heart years before I found the courage to write it all down. It's a book that stayed in my mind and haunted my body for years while I grew up. It's a book that came to be in a spacious room somewhere in northern Illinois and was recited aloud to no one in an underground Williamsburg apartment. It's a book that was written on warm Miami beaches, painted in a small, loving studio in East Nashville, Tennessee, and shaped by a sixteen-bedroom Victorian commune in Berkeley, California. It's a book that was born from a year of complete heartbreak and loneliness in Crown Heights, Brooklyn.

This is a book that asks you to look in the mirror without flinching. You won't always like what you see. That's okay. Look anyway.

This is a book that wants to be held. These pages are filled with honesty, and, I hope, some grace. My greatest wish is that you will find them useful.

This book admits that everything changes. There's no use in holding on to sunshine or sorrow; with time, one melts into the other. Like you, both can be reborn.

This is a book that was written to remind you of one thing:

YOU ARE NOT ALONE.

FIRST, SAY TO YOURSELF

BE; & THEN DO

HAVE

WHAT YOU WOULD

WHAT YOU

TO DO.

- EPICTETUS

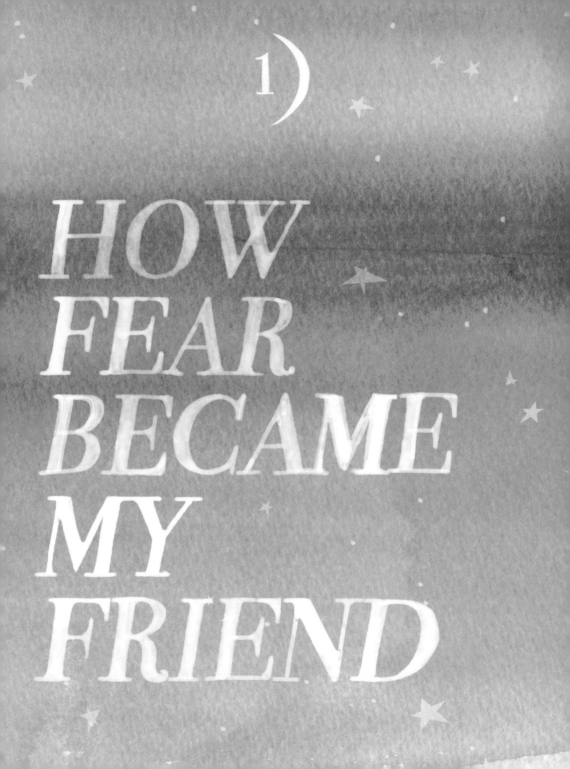

1

HOW FEAR BECAME MY FRIEND

Like everyone, I came into this world without fear.

I was born with no concepts of desire or consequence, only a deep hunger for newness and all five senses intact—to see, smell, hear, touch, taste—to experience as many things as possible in the hours after my eyes open and before they again close.

I want to feel.

The morning sun is warm and makes me more alive. It feels like a soft blanket that follows me throughout the day. In the afternoon it burns brighter and more fiercely still, and I wonder how much closer it's gotten to Earth. I'm hot and a bit uncomfortable, but I want to know how much I can endure. I test my physical and emotional boundaries and push them to expand. If my curiosity has a limit, it has never presented itself to me, and I've never once asked to see it. I like to explore.

I want to know.

In the evening, I see the stars slowly come out and wonder how these little stones can be so far away and still leave such deep wonder inside me. I want to know how the moon carves away at itself night after night until there is nothing left. Constellations connect themselves behind my eyes, and I feel that there is meaning behind every movement happening around me. In my dreams, I ask the world: Is this the magic? Have I finally found it?

I want to understand.

When I'm very young, the questions are large: What happens
in the time that I'm asleep? When I close my eyes, where do
I go? Is each day a new life or just a different story on a
different line on the same page in the same book? What color
is the book? How many pages does it have? I go to bed each
night hoping the book is very long. I'm in constant awe of the
simple fact that there is a game called life and I was given
the chance to play it. Maybe this is the magic.

When I'm a little older, the questions change slightly. By now, I've discovered myself: Why do I look the way I do and why isn't it the way everyone else does? Why doesn't Caitlin want to play with me? How come I'm the only one in school who speaks two languages?

The answers are too complicated for my four-year-old brain, but my native tongue moves inside my mouth and words tumble out before I've had the chance to consider them. They make the right sounds anyway. I marvel at my own ability to speak and think and listen. I move like water— my hand rises before my mind has even fully given the command, before the answer is even in my mouth, because I trust that my thoughts will finish forming before I'm called on.

Everything feels so connected.
My brain is an athlete: lightning-fast
and powerful, capable of anything.
I can do anything.

This is the magic.

As an adult, I've found it fairly difficult to hold on to magic.

Not long after I was marveling at my own ability to exist—
to simply float and feel and be a speck in an ever-expanding
universe—did I stumble onto another plane, one where
contentment turned to anxiety and innate ability turned to
doubt.

I've spent the greater amount of my life living in fear.
My fear is multitudinous: it begins as one thing and ends up
as another, splitting itself into one million pieces that scatter
off into every direction. It exists both inside and outside of
myself, and follows me around the way I wished my older
sister always would (she never did).

There are many fears inside me, but mostly there is the fear
of being different—a fear so large and magnanimous that it
has never left my side. It comes from knowing that my body
is different from anyone else's. It's different from yours.
My color is different. It's golden sometimes, toasty in the
winter, and a deep, burnt caramel when I'm in the sun for too
long. My ethnicity makes me different, as does my culture,
my language. As I've gotten older, my native tongue has quieted,
so much so that I now fumble over the words. Instead, I speak
English because it lets me blend into my surroundings.
It doesn't give other people a reason to look at me quizzically—
in fact, speaking English allows me to slip by unnoticed.
If you don't look too closely, I'm a blur—inseparable from the
elements to the left or right of me. For a lot of my life,
I've tried to remain out of focus.

The FEAR OF BEING DIFFERENT forces me
to be like everyone else.

Being pulled apart by fear is a continual surprise and often makes me wonder where I went wrong: If I had done things differently, would it still be here? If I were a better person, surely I'd be traveling the world carelessly, forging wonderful friendships with ease, experiencing more than I ever dreamed possible. I wouldn't be sitting in a coffee shop in downtown Chicago, utterly stricken by fear—would I? The answer, of course, is yes: fear would still be here. It would be here even if I said the right words or showed up on time, even if everything went exactly according to plan.

Fear will still be here because fear is not a consequence—it's not a punishment we receive for doing something wrong or behaving badly. It is not something that we feel because we lack the strength to overcome it—in fact, fear isn't an obstacle to overcome at all. Fear is a light that's meant to guide us. It builds strength and provides sustenance. It has the ability to split us open like a knife does a pomegranate, spilling seeds of beauty and incredible possibility from the inside.

There are moments when I simply feel free. Untethered from my constant fear of being different, of being judged or singled out. In these moments, I float.

Close your eyes and imagine yourself floating down a quiet stream. The water feels cool and familiar, like it was made to gently support your body. Wildlife shimmers and sways around you. Birds flutter and butterflies join them. Clouds make their way across the sky like they were meant to. There's nothing for you to do but float. *I belong here,* you think to yourself.

Freedom is the recognition that where you are right now is exactly where you're supposed to be. It's fear that has reminded me, over and over again, that yes, I am different—from you or anyone else—and how lucky I am that this is so. It's fear that has forced me to turn my ideas of difference over in my head until I could see that difference is beautiful—that I am lucky to be one-of-a-kind, and that these very differences are what have allowed me to thrive.

Fear is a friend, and it's here to support you. Like all friendships, the one you have with fear is a two-way street. It requires time, hard work, and honesty in order to become and remain healthy. It requires us to sit with it, listen to it, and try our best to understand it—even though we don't always know how. Like any friend, fear can help you only if you let it.

In the throes of darkness, fear makes us feel as if magic doesn't exist—but what if it's actually telling us exactly where to find it? Think back to a few moments ago, when you were floating down that quiet stream. The water gurgles and splashes around you. There is a breeze, and when it touches you, you feel safe. Remember what it's like to feel free.

Fear is always beside us, but it doesn't keep us from freedom: it leads us to it, slowly moving us toward the magic.

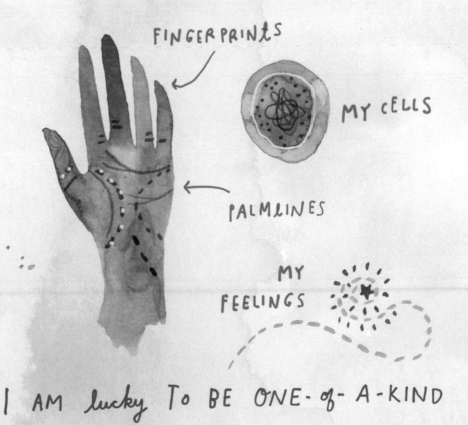

FINGERPRINTS

MY CELLS

PALMLINES

MY FEELINGS

I AM lucky To BE ONE-of-A-KIND

THOSE WHO DON'T BELIEVE IN *magic* WILL NEVER FIND IT.

ROALD DAHL

29

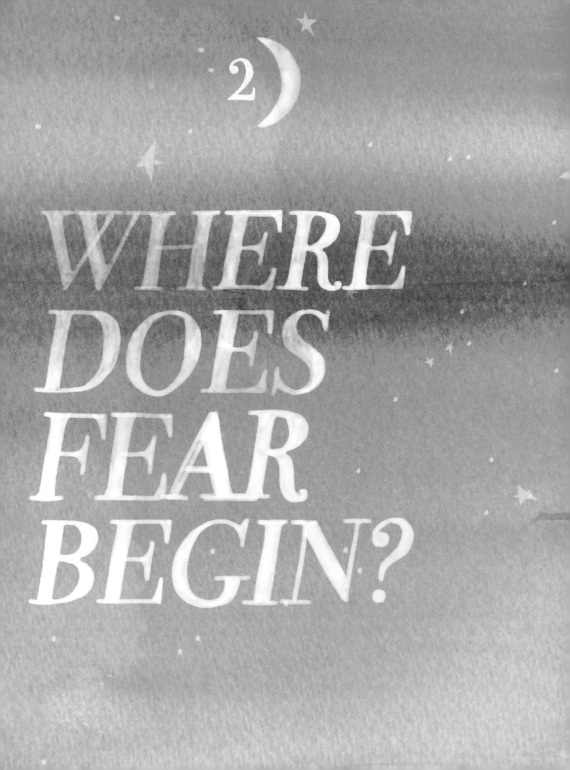

2

WHERE DOES FEAR BEGIN?

We are born fearless. We are born free.

As we grow older, our affinity for curiosity dampens in favor of security—the ability to feel safe and cared for. Though each person's life and environment is varied, there are a few permanent stones that offer security: acceptance, understanding, community, love, and freedom. When we don't have these stones in place, or when one of them is endangered, fear leaps in to fill the vacancy. It replaces the feeling of safety with anxiety. Our minds are uneasy, filled with confusion. We don't know what to do next. Where do we go from here?

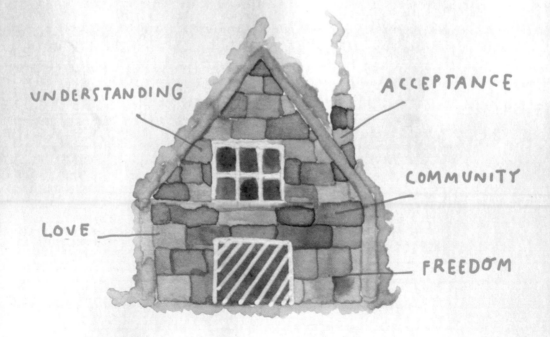

Like all other emotions, fear is born in the mind. It's rooted in our brains, the same magical instrument that fills us with wonder, awe, and incomprehensible joy. What prompts fear to take birth in us changes constantly. Its birth is dependent on our circumstances and abilities to lasso our emotions, but one thing is certain: fear did not arrive here, in our minds, on its own.

Our culture tells us to be afraid—afraid of the powerful and afraid of being vulnerable, afraid of money (because it corrupts) and afraid of poverty (because it stifles). Our culture tells us to be afraid of what we are (human!) and who we innately are (our honest, most beautiful selves). We are continually told that changing ourselves is the only way we'll ever be accepted, loved, cherished, or seen.

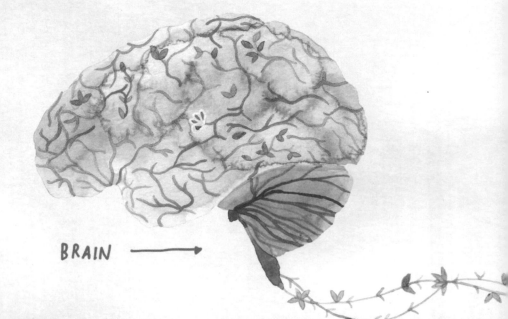

BRAIN ⟶

I live in New York, so I ride the train daily. I always look at the subway ads, which reflect what our culture is preoccupied with at the moment. There are usually advertisements for plastic surgery featuring women who are so much happier now that they've modified their bodies. I roll my eyes at these signs, but inside I feel uneasy. *Am I supposed to look like that?* I silently wonder to myself, staring at my reflection in the train windows. I'm not even close. The wall in front of me features a cosmetic company that prides itself on creating the most natural-looking makeup. I'm not convinced it's more natural than the bare face I wear, but the girls in the ad look beautiful. *It wouldn't hurt to put some mascara on before leaving the house*, I tell myself, awakening insecurities that were asleep before I'd stepped onto the subway. I don't want plastic surgery, but I do have a fear of not being beautiful. I don't enjoy wearing makeup, but I do have a fear of not fitting in.

FEAR

I know where these fears came from, but it doesn't mean grappling with them is easy. Modern culture paints fear as a dark, powerful thing that has the ability to control us—but fear isn't the true culprit here. It isn't fear that tells us to change who we are—it's our culture—the signs, voices, and messages we're surrounded by.

FEAR of LOSS

fear of NOT BEING LIKED

fear of being UNLOVED

FEAR of BEING FEARFUL

As we grow older, these fears grow with us, morphing and dividing themselves into hundreds of other fears until it's impossible to locate where it all began. Rationally, I know that being beautiful isn't reserved for a singular body type, but it's difficult to remember when the world repeatedly tells me otherwise. If I take a moment to understand it, I can see how my fear of being unattractive to others has created several other fears: the fear of unacceptance, the fear of never being loved, the fear of rejection. These are all tied up together like a bouquet of fears, and when I feel unattractive, they all bloom inside me.

fear of being
REJECTED

fear
of FAILURE

FEAR *of* LONELINESS

Most of the time, we don't create our own fears—we carry other people's fears within us. Parents, often unknowingly, are the first people who begin unloading their fears onto their children. In order to protect them, parents instill a fear of foreignness in their babies. They ask them to stay close. They teach them to follow the same path they once took, because the path's familiarity offers safety. The crevices are known. If there are shortcuts, they can be shared. Why choose winding and circuitous when you can go straight?

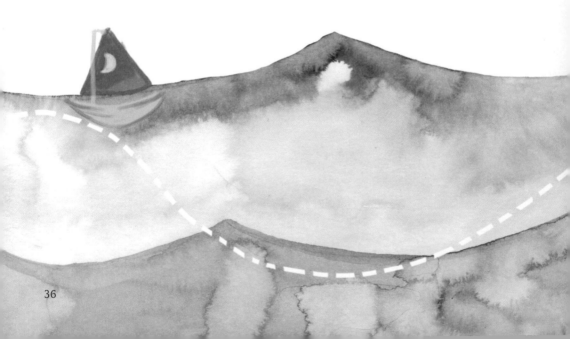

This is usually done with the purest of intention: parents want to protect their children from pain and difficulty. They want to give us the value of the lessons they've learned so we won't have to learn them ourselves. This usually backfires because as children, we do learn by example, but we learn best from experience. Cautious warnings shape themselves into fears, and these fears then prevent us from trying new things, including experiences that can fulfill and fortify us. We miss out on the necessary experiences that can shape us into the people we most want to be.

My parents immigrated to the United States from India when they were in their late twenties and carefully built a beautiful life together. Their approach was pragmatic because they were both born into poverty. They had no money and no wild wishes—only to cross a cold, wide ocean to an unknown land and live more healthily and happily than they had before.

As a child, I was loved fiercely and protectively. I was loved by two people who knew what it was like to have nothing, and it was under their protection that I learned how to live in scarcity.

The idea that all good things come at a cost is a tenet of the scarcity mind-set. Scarcity taught me that there weren't enough opportunities for everyone, and that the more success others had, the less there would be for me. When I thought about who I wasn't, my heart beat faster. What if I never became the person the world wanted me to be? Maybe my spirit didn't sparkle enough. Or was it that it sparkled too much?

All I felt was fear. In fact, I couldn't remember the last time I felt unafraid.

WHEN
THE LA
YOU
UNAF

WAS

ST TIME

FELT

RAID?

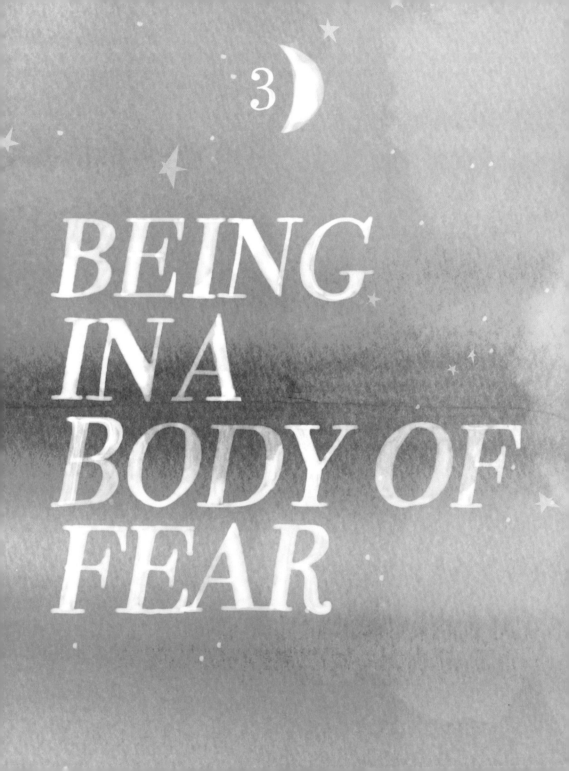

3

BEING IN A BODY OF FEAR

The most complicated fears we harbor and hold on to are the ones that begin and end with who we are. It's easy to pick ourselves apart for things we cannot control, but the truth is that most of life happens outside of our control. It's impossible to make someone love you (or leave you), change the body you were born into, or choose the circumstances that surround you.

I was afraid of myself for a long time. I spent a whole summer lying in bed, watching the ceiling fan whir above me. The air, thick and wet, lowered itself onto me like thousands of soggy, thin blankets, the way August air in New York always does. It was a Saturday morning. What I really wished I could do was go to the beach—but the very idea kept me from getting up.

Everything around me buzzed with the excitement of summer in the city. The sidewalks were filled with outdoor brunches and breezy dresses, and the subways were crowded with my sun-starved neighbors, headed to Coney Island or Long Island for a relaxing day far away from the headaches and stresses of city life.

I thought about showering and putting on a bathing suit. *It won't be so bad,* I told myself, but my heartbeat was already picking up speed. I thought about putting on a pair of shorts and stepping outside into the sunlight. Into the big, bright world. I wanted to feel the warmth against my skin, but my chest was beginning to tighten and my eyebrows were knitted together, considering all the things that could easily go wrong. My mind drowned with possibilities, all simultaneously pushing and pulling, overwhelming me as they spiraled out of control. What I really wanted to do was go to the beach—but my fear wouldn't let me.

Fear is born in the mind but it quickly begins to form a physical shape. It is closely entwined with the nervous system and when awakened, sends a clear message to the brain: *Help. I'm in danger.*

Inside the body, adrenaline surges—first through the brain, encouraging you to make impulsive, split-second decisions, then through your arms and legs, preparing you to escape the imagined danger in front of you. In order to keep up with the body's demands, your heart pumps blood harder and faster, forcing shallow breaths to come more quickly. The idea that everything will be okay becomes unfathomable.

For me, this is what it felt like when I thought about going to the beach.

Ever since I became aware of beauty and its value to the world, the idea of going to the beach has made me stiff with anxiety. By the time I was six months old, I'd had two corrective surgeries, leaving me with a seventeen-inch scar that snakes its way along the inside of my foot and up the back of my leg. Like a lot of scars, it looks like a poorly placed zipper. Like anything that makes us different, it brought a lot of fear into my life—and it started at the beach.

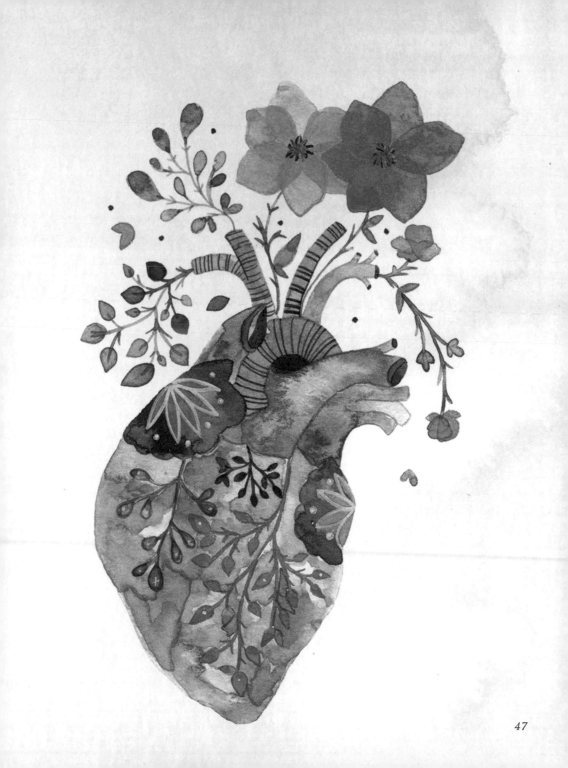

One day I was practicing how to float in saltwater, and on the very next day I threw out all of my bathing suits. I'd learned to recognize myself as different. My friends averted their eyes when I wore shorts. My other classmates were far less kind. A boy said he'd heard about my body, the way my legs were different and ugly. He wanted to know what was wrong with me. I wanted to say that there was nothing wrong with me, but no words came out.

By the time I reached age twelve, I'd left the beach behind. It wasn't a place for me.

I wanted to feel the salt on my skin, in my hair, the hollowness that enters my lungs after spending too much time in the water. I wanted to remember the sun looking down on the sea, light fractals reflecting like thousands of mirrors lining the horizon. I wanted to collect a memory of myself completely immersed in the magic of it all—light, water, body all as one, pressed so closely together that I could no longer find where I ended and the ocean began. I wanted to remember feeling free.

Instead, I thought about bathing suits. Bikini or one-piece,
boy shorts, or string? No matter what I chose, someone would
see the scar—and I'd feel their eyes seeing it. I briefly
considered the option of a wetsuit, all too aware that the idea
was as ridiculous as the fear that kept me indoors.

I thought about bodies and their imperfections and why we
carry them around as unforgivable symbols of who we really
are. I thought about my legs and how often I've wanted to
trade them in for another set, a forgettable pair. I've wanted to
fade into the background for years.

Lying in bed was safe. The ceiling fan spun. I knew exactly what would happen next, how this day would turn into tomorrow and then the one after that. Sometimes fear is imperceptible, a ghost that sits quietly next to me. Sometimes it looks at me and I can see right through it, see how it tricks me into believing in something that isn't really there. Other times, fear is the dust on my ceiling fan: dark and rooted, deeply hoping that I'll never acknowledge it.

I wondered how long before the inability to accept myself and my body would become a memory, an unrecognizable face, someone I used to know.

How long WOULD IT BE before I FINALLY FELT Comfortable BEING SEEN?

4

SAY HELLO TO FEAR

We are not alone in our fears. Look around you: every person you see is afraid of something. Some are small fears (losing our keys) and some are large (losing a loved one), but they live inside each one of us. Many of the fears we carry are justified, but many, many more begin as reasonable concerns before quickly evolving into irrational beasts.

Our brain is designed to protect us. It doesn't always know the difference between facing a hungry shark or saying hello to a stranger. It's up to us to teach it the difference.

Sit with your fears.

Tune into your fears. Are you able to separate the irrational fears from the rational ones? Which fears scare you the most?

When you feel fear coming closer, ask yourself: Where is it coming from? What is its root—is it sprouting from my present circumstances or does it not have any root at all?

FEAR
of JUMPING INTO WATER

← FEAR

FEAR of DROWNING

← FEAR

← root
(can't swim)

Irrational fears are stories that we weave into long, spinning tales. We tell these stories to ourselves repeatedly, choosing colors and feelings to accompany each twist, creating entire paintings of how each story will unfortunately unfold. These stories live in the future, always wondering what happens next, while rational fears live in the present. Identifying whether your current fear has a root can quickly help you to determine which kind of fear it is.

fear OF
BEING HURT AGAIN

fear OF
NEVER BEING LOVED   FEAR

root

FEAR

(history of toxic
relationships)

Listen to fear's story.

Identify the purpose behind your fear. What will you accomplish if you quiet this irrational fear?

Irrational fears paralyze us. They prevent us from being present in our daily lives, from honestly connecting with one another, and from being who we really are.

SMALL LIFE

We often sensationalize how unfortunate the endings to our stories are—we believe our potential pain is boundless and will ultimately ruin us. Change the story that your fear tells you. Instead of focusing on the fantastic-but-ultimately-imaginary pain your fear is saving you from, look at what your irrational fears do to you: they force you to live a small life instead of discovering the incredible world waiting for you.

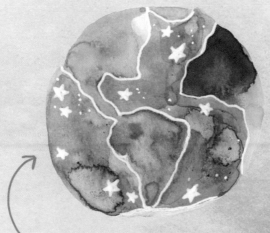

INCREDIBLE WORLD
WAITING FOR YOU

in moments of fear,
i always come to a
FAMILIAR CROSSROAD:
i can fold and live
a little more safely,
with QUIETNESS instead
of conflict, or i can
GO ON and TRY,
knowing there is no promise
of SAFETY or TRIUMPH
waiting for me.

60

these two choices stare
at me knowingly, because
no matter how many times
i've come face to face with
them, i've always chosen the
same one. I CHOOSE TO
KEEP TRYING. i choose to
keep trying even when
i don't want to. I FAN
THE LITTLE FLAME INSIDE ME
and KEEP IT FROM GOING OUT
ONCE MORE.

Take one by the hand.

Find things that scare you. Let them scare you. Do them anyway.

If you're afraid of venturing to unfamiliar places, try taking a different route to work. When that becomes easier, make plans to visit a different part of your city. This becomes extra special if it's a place you've always wanted to go—a museum, café, or concert—but haven't because you were afraid.

MOVING to
ANOTHER COUNTRY

MAKING ART
NO ONE LIKES

swimming
in the ocean

If your irrational fear is of judgment or discomfort from others, say hello to the person in front of you in line at the coffee shop. Compliment someone you pass on the street. Give others the opportunity to help you lessen your fears. If there's anything I've learned while overcoming this fear myself, it's that people will always surprise you if you let them. Life is nothing other than a brilliant collection of experiences—some rough, many smooth, some found under water, others under stone. Look for them all. They're yours to take.

talking to
strangers

BEING
ALONE

letting someone
see my heart

losing myself

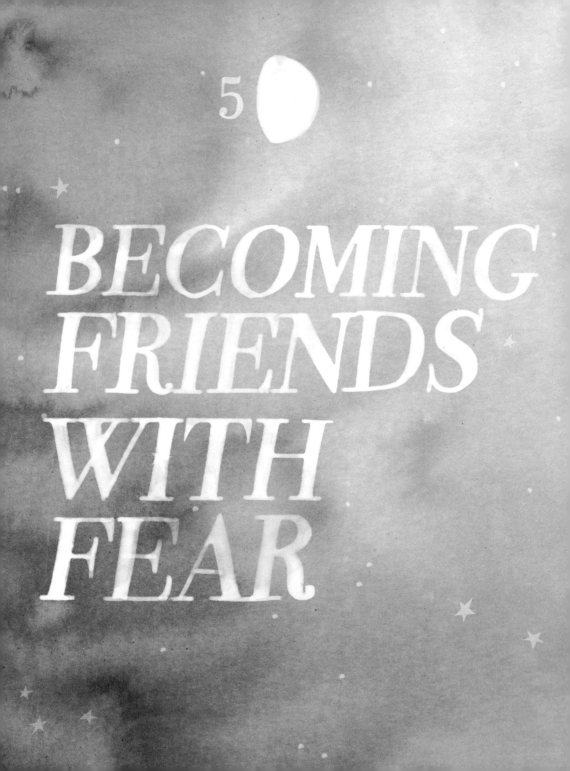

5

BECOMING FRIENDS WITH FEAR

I let fear scare me for years because I didn't know how to see
it for what it really was: my closest friend. Fear is someone
who knows me well, who knows each dream and longing
and what prevents me from going after them. Fear knows who
I want to be and what keeps me from being that person.
Fear knows where I want to go and what stops me from taking
each step.

Fear is my closest friend. I have said the words aloud to myself
many times.

Fear is my closest friend. Once I accepted this, something began to shift. For the first time, I was able to take a step back from myself and recognize what was happening. Becoming aware of fear is the first step to befriending it. After all, how can you become friends with something you're pretending doesn't exist?

Every time I felt scared—instead of letting my anxieties build up and take over my body—I took the first step and asked myself a question I'd always avoided:

AM I AFRAID?

The answer was yes.

Accepting your fears is the only way to overcome them.
Fear isn't something that wants to stay hidden inside you,
preventing you from moving forward. Fear wants to quietly
shine beside you, helping you find your path. Becoming aware
of why you are afraid is the next step. So, I began asking
myself a second question:

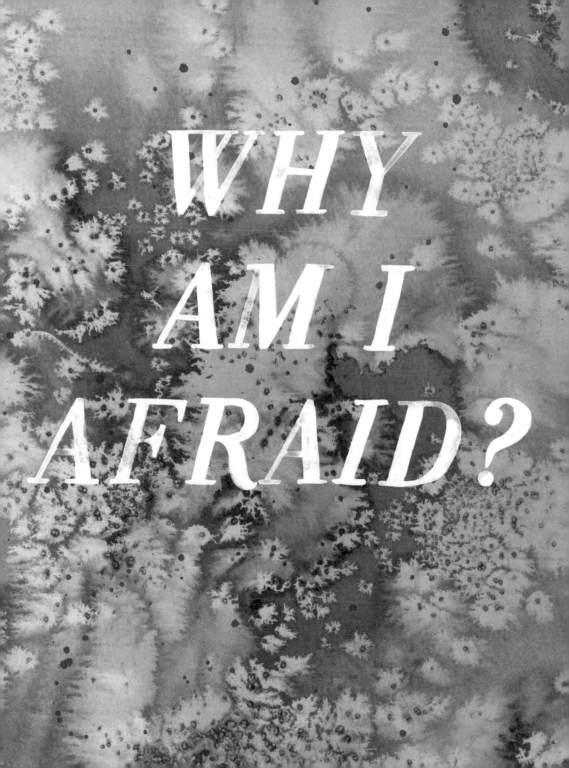

I was afraid of not fitting in. My whole life, I'd let my scars replace who I was. When fear came to visit, it brought with it anxiety and a deep air of discomfort and nervousness— feelings that made it impossible for me to recognize myself. Rejection, based on the assumption of what everyone else thought of me, became all encompassing, a dark maze I couldn't find my way out of.

I was afraid of being judged. I was afraid of being unloved. I was afraid of being an outsider.

My fear grew and grew until it became larger than me. It loomed over me like a monster, a bewildering, frightening beast that threatened to never leave. When I looked in the mirror, I didn't see myself: I saw only my scars. Instead of seeing something that made me special and stronger, I saw something that separated me from everyone else.

Fear changes what you see in front of you, but I was learning that how I perceived that change—whether I saw something negative or positive, something that would help or harm—was up to me. I knew I was afraid. I knew why I was afraid. This brought me to my third question:

Nothing.

It's okay to be afraid. All it means is that there's something you care deeply about. It's okay to have fears, as long as you are willing to explore them. It's okay to hug fear closely, to poke and prod and discover what's underneath that heavy, dark cloak.

The reason it's so hard to see fear as a friend is that we let it remind us of what we don't want instead of what we do. I wanted to fit in, I wanted to be loved, I wanted to be accepted. I was afraid of never having those things, but I wasn't even giving myself a chance to find them. I wanted to be on a path, but I was afraid of walking. I had to take the first step, and I had to take it with fear by my side, instead of in front of me, blocking my path.

So I began walking. I walked with fear for a long time.
I let myself feel anxious, I let the darkness cover me.
My heartbeats rapidly increased and then slowed back down.
I became comfortable with the fact that there was something
that I was afraid of. The more I walked with fear, the more
that fear itself changed.

Being brave, being courageous is not living a life without great
fear—it's seeing fear clearly and living a greater life with it
beside you. It's breathing deeply and allowing your fear to
breathe the same air. It's knowing that you aren't alone, even if
no one is next to you. It's realizing that you have the power to
choose which fears will guide you, and which are better left
behind.

Although I was afraid of being rejected, I was more afraid of never letting myself be accepted. I was afraid of being unloved, but I was more afraid of never giving myself the chance to be loved. I was afraid of being an outsider, but I was more afraid of never letting someone see me.

Lying in bed was safe, but it would never surprise me. I wanted to move forward, knowing that there were unimaginable wonders ahead. I wanted to be on a path, and I wanted it to lead somewhere else. I was tired of being here. So what if I was afraid?

I went to the beach. The air was salty and the water was clear. So what if my heart fluttered a bit while I approached the wild sea? The waves crashed into each other, reflecting the light of an unbelievable sun. So what if my heartbeat quickened while I stripped down to my bathing suit?

The sun warmed me as the water
rushed around my ankles.

I was
free.

6

FEAR IS HERE TO HELP YOU:
Uncover Your Greatest Wish

What is your

FINDING MY LIFE PARTNER

SEEING THE
NATURAL WORLD

BEING HAPPY
WITH WHERE I AM

FRIENDSHIPS THAT LAST

w

e

s

greatest wish?

ACCEPTING MYSELF

KNOWING WHAT DIRECTION TO MOVE FORWARD IN

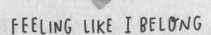

FEELING LIKE I BELONG

What is your greatest wish? Is it to find your life partner? Is it to start your own family? Is it to build a career that you love and are successful in? Is it to travel wildly and experience more of the natural world?

When you dare to identify your greatest desire, the possibility of falling short sneaks in beside it. This is why voicing any wish aloud feels risky: saying, *Yes, I really want this,* opens us up to the possibility of disappointment and failure before we've even begun to reach up toward the dream. If we're not careful, our fear can overshadow our desire.

The impostor syndrome is a common example—the fear that our achievements aren't deserved, that underneath our progress and success we're actually fraudulent and unworthy.

When we receive a raise or promotion at work, we believe we simply "got lucky"—it couldn't possibly be that our efforts and determination finally paid off. When success comes to us, we believe it came unearned. We feel guilty instead of proud. Didn't someone else work harder and do more? Don't they deserve this more than we do?

IMPOSTOR SYNDROME

While this particular fear will do everything in its power to dismiss your successes, it also highlights your most intimate wish: to be a caring parent, a successful writer, or a trusted friend. The impostor syndrome affects those of us who wish to be of value—not because we are ego-driven, but because we want to believe that we have something to offer.

Our doubt comes from our desire.

When you feel the impostor syndrome coming on, invite it to sit beside you. Close your eyes and feel the waves of self-doubt vibrate through your bones. Slowly, let them soften and subside. Watch carefully as the guilt you feel outlines the things you care about most in this world, and feel gratitude for your ability to discern what makes you feel alive. This is not easy work, but it is essential. Like all other fears, the impostor syndrome has two faces: one that can help and one that can harm. Which you choose to see is up to you.

7

FEAR'S MANY FACES

Fear is a primitive emotion our bodies designed to keep us safe, and it affects the entire animal world, not just people. When sensing a possible threat, the brain translates it as a warning. We react with fear, signaling to our bodies that we need to escape to safety.

As the human species continued to evolve, so did our fear. Originally resulting in a simple fight-or-flight response, fear has become a complicated, winding emotion that now bears paralyzing secondary emotions like guilt, despair, and shame—things most of us experience on a daily basis. Unlike core emotions, like anger and joy, which envelop us vigorously and dissipate just as quickly, the complex symptoms of compounded emotions like *guilt* (a combination of fear + joy), *despair* (fear + sadness), and *shame* (fear + disgust) linger and slowly take root in our bones. Many people feel the effects of fear through guilt, despair, and shame for extended periods of time, often lasting for weeks or even years.

THEORY OF

ANTICIPATION

ANGER

DISGUST

SADNESS

BASIC EMOTIONS

JOY

TRUST

FEAR

SURPRISE

Shame and the power it holds over us.

Shame is the least-discussed emotion that stems from fear, and its debilitating effects quickly magnify because it isolates us. Fear of judgment leaves us feeling ashamed of our actions, beliefs, feelings—or simply who we are. We know that we're supposed to love ourselves despite the shortcomings everyone tells us we have, but it can be hard to hear the sound of your own voice among the many others in your head. Back in my Brooklyn bedroom, I ignored the one confident voice inside me that assured me my body was beautiful, choosing instead to listen to the many that told me it wasn't.

being a stay-at-home parent

being a working parent

shame

spending

saving

shame

hiding

vulnerability

shame

Because we feel disgusted by our own shame or lack of self-love, we often don't communicate our feelings to anyone. Instead, we silently sit in the emotion, enabling the waves of shame to grow stronger until we slip beneath them. The longer we rest in any one emotion, the stronger its hold is over us, and the more muted our other emotions become. It becomes impossible to trust or believe that we are of value—to believe that we're worthy of anything other than the awful state we're in. If someone tells us that we're beautiful, we feel skeptical because we don't believe the truth in their words.

And then: guilt sweeps in because we don't believe the sentiment is something we deserve.

Fear gains strength through anxiety.

Anxiety is the combination of fear and anticipation, and it visits many of us regularly. It's often mistaken for fear itself, because the two share many physical symptoms: a quickened heartbeat, shallow breathing, and cyclical thoughts competing for attention in our minds. But anxiety is not fear—it's our anticipation of what we most fear coming to fruition. A person with a fear of loneliness becomes anxious at the thought of breaking up with their partner or refuses to spend a weekend alone. A person with a fear of failure becomes anxious at the prospect of trying anything new.

For the past two years, a close friend of mine has been working toward a graduate degree as an early-childhood teacher. She's a compassionate and caring person, a natural caregiver. When she recently graduated, I told her how proud I was of her and asked if she felt relieved. I was surprised to learn that she wasn't. Despite graduating with a 4.0 GPA and stellar recommendations, she felt anxious: What if she didn't get a job? What if she wasn't a good teacher? What if her students didn't feel cared for? As soon as she graduated, she began carrying with her the well-being of hundreds of children she hadn't even met yet, everywhere she went. Her anxiety wasn't always center stage, but it shadowed her continuously. The weight was heavy. She hadn't begun teaching yet, but her shoulders were already tired.

Most of our greatest fears have never materialized, but we still continue to believe in them. We let fear splinter into despair and guilt and shame, not considering the way these emotions take residence in our body, moving into the homes where confidence, contentment, and self-worth used to live.

It's easy to resign ourselves to our fears, especially when we begin to accept them as an unchangeable fact of our daily lives. *I'm so happy I'm not an anxious person,* I often tell myself, but in moments of self-awareness, it's clear that as the soundtrack to my life, my anxieties are always playing in the background. Sometimes the volume is low enough that I can barely hear it, but the music is always there.

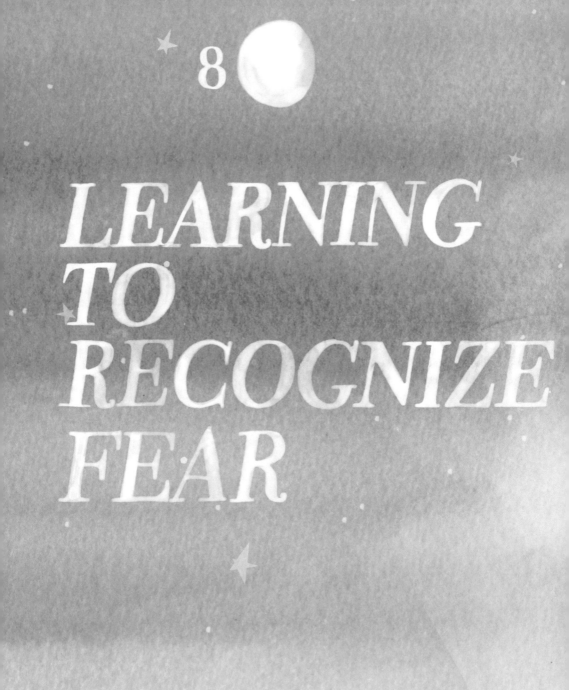

8

LEARNING TO RECOGNIZE FEAR

The single greatest step we can take to change the position fear plays in our lives is also the most essential: learning to see it when it appears. This sounds easy, but as humans, our species is notorious for failing to recognize truths that are usually right in front of us. The fastest way to summon your fear at any time is simple: all you need to do is look at yourself.

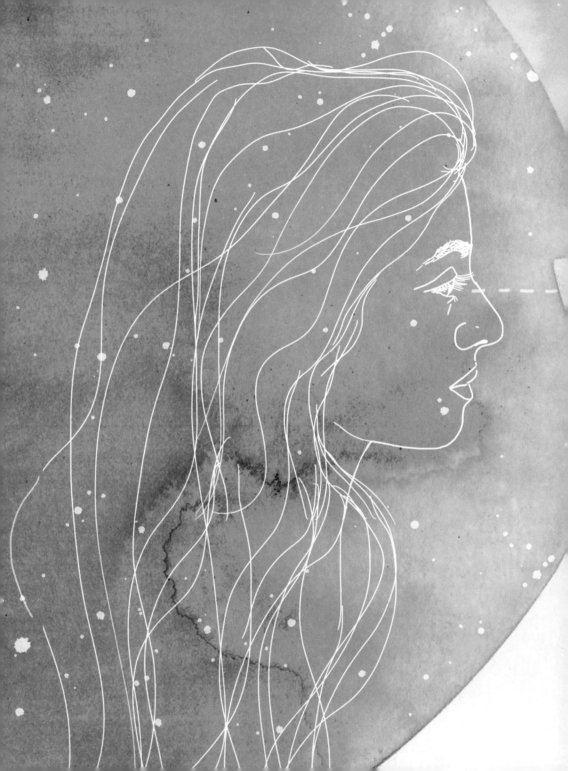

Italian psychologist Giovanni Caputo studied people looking into the mirror for ten minutes at a time, concentrating on nothing other than their own faces. Instead of seeing their faces as they truly are, people experienced a variety of visual illusions: two-thirds of individuals saw a deformed version of themselves, and one-fifth saw a distorted parent's face in the mirror; nearly half of all patients saw an extraordinarily monstrous being staring back at them. Caputo found that 100 percent of people experienced some form of dissociative identity disorder—meaning that at some point during the experiment, each person failed to recognize the person in the mirror as themselves.

There are truths hidden inside all of us, and because they are painful to see, we keep them buried under layers of flesh and bone, choosing instead to never look at them. Most of the time, we pretend our fear doesn't exist, but it does—and like the reflections in Caputo's experiment, sometimes it appears in startling ways.

What does my fear look like?

In an effort to see our fear a little more closely, place yourself in front of a mirror and look into your own eyes. Is there anything you're trying not to see? After I look into my own eyes long enough, I see vulnerability in the childlike qualities my face has yet to lose, the small person inside me who feels forgotten. Vulnerability is something I'm afraid to see because I often cast it as weakness, even now. Fear can look like a sharp memory you haven't forgotten. It can look like confusion, static, like the thoughts that have stopped moving inside your head. Is it very difficult not to look away? Maybe fear looks like self-loathing if what you're afraid of most is loving yourself.

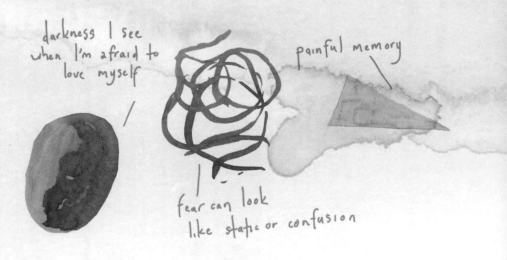

darkness I see when I'm afraid to love myself

painful memory

fear can look like static or confusion

Now, close your eyes. What does fear look like now? Maybe, like the people in Caputo's study, you see a distorted version of yourself, or a variation of someone you know well. Does fear look like a void, nothing but darkness? Fear comes in every color. Does it move in waves across your mind's hemisphere, fading from pink to blue to white? Do you see reds and oranges burning behind your eyes, or is fear a cool black, smooth and velvet, beckoning you to stay still?

Spend time looking at your fear and observing the different forms it comes in. As you begin recognizing them, you'll become more comfortable looking at yourself, even though it means acknowledging fears that you wish weren't there. Each fear is connected to a piece of you that holds a wish, a dream, a hope—and like the blood that runs through us, each wish is essential to making us who we are.

fear moves in waves

every fear is connected to a wish or hope I have

nothingness

What does my fear feel like?

When fear approaches us, we usually avoid meeting its glance, and when it reaches toward us, we do our best to avoid its touch—but in order to really understand our fear, we have to examine how it feels.

a heat that flushes through me

quickening pulse, increased heart rate

The next time you feel fear, draw it closer. Hug yourself when you feel it rattling inside you. Fear can feel like a heavy heartbeat inside your chest, each smack against your breastbone increasing in frequency and strength. Your pulse quickens as you feel adrenaline sprinting through your body, pounding against your shoulders, wrists, to the very tips of each finger. Is it a heat, slow and flushed, creeping up to your collar like a fever? Or does it make you shiver and tense up until you're no longer able to move?

Fear dissolves through recognition. Understanding the way fear physically affects your body will help you to alleviate its symptoms next time it appears. The darkness in fear is a mirage, and like any magic trick, it loses power once you understand how the trick works.

small shivers that
tense my body —

— adrenaline rushes
through my body

What does my fear sound like?

Listening is meditation, and it is often the quickest way to quiet your fear—the more you understand the sounds, the less there is to be afraid of. Tune in to your heartbeat. What sound does your heart make as it pounds faster against your chest—a loud knock or a smaller, steadier drumming? Does your breath heave from your chest as your fear grows, or does it become shallow, small gasps that search for escape?

Does fear fill your mind with the panicked chatter of hundreds of what-ifs, or does it eliminate all possibilities, filling your mind with the sounds of silence? My fear leads me to create and explore the unlikeliest of outcomes, no matter how ridiculous they are, until my mind is too exhausted to consider logic.

How many voices are inside your head? When we're feeling fearful, the various tongues of our fear begin speaking at once. One voice becomes many, and our internal monologue quickly loses itself in the din. Does one belong to a parent or sibling that you're afraid of disappointing? Does one belong to the self-critic who says you aren't good or enough? Does one belong to your peers, or a culture that says you need to be different?

Just as you would trust a friend to tell you the truth, begin a conversation with fear and listen carefully to what it says.

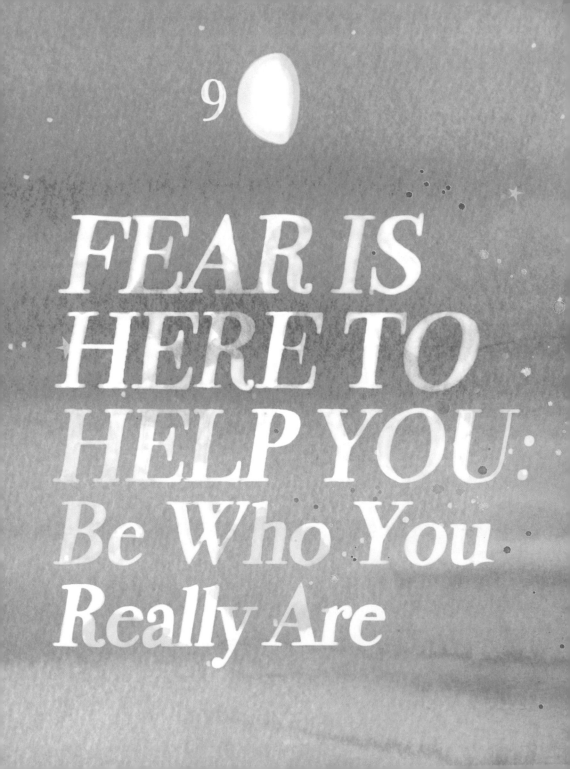

9

FEAR IS HERE TO HELP YOU:
Be Who You Really Are

BE WHO YOU REALLY ARE-

YOUR TRUE, UNADULTERATED SELF.

All too often, we self-censor in an effort to avoid being seen as Other. We suppress our laughter because we're worried it's too loud. We avoid answering honestly when someone asks us how we are because the truth makes us feel uncomfortable. The process of self-censorship eventually becomes second nature until it no longer feels like you're actively hiding: your laugh was always this quiet; you always feel just fine. Over time, we hardly recognize who we are.

When I first started painting, I didn't know where to begin. I studied the angles of the faces famous artists drew and mimicked the lines in my mind. I didn't dare use paper and ink. I didn't want to try. I knew I wouldn't like the results.

I wondered why color palettes didn't come instinctively to me—why was I drawn to raw reds and blues instead of muted sea foam and yellow? Why didn't I know exactly what to do with a blank canvas? Why wasn't anything I painted pretty? Why couldn't I just open up and let amazing work fall out of me?

MY COLOR
PALEtte \

Being unsure of myself didn't feel good, but it was easy.
It meant that I didn't have to figure out who I was or what my
work said about me. It meant that instead of listening to
myself, I could just listen to everyone else. I had a lot of
practice doing that.

I'm a self-taught artist. I didn't go to art school, and I certainly
didn't know how to make money by painting. For a while
I painted portraits because that's what people wanted—family
portraits, wedding portraits, and even pet portraits. I painted
portraits because people paid me for them, and I believed that
the measure of a successful artist was determined by money.
I painted realistically instead of freely because I believed that
technical skill was the mark of a true artist. In both cases,
I was wrong. I placed the value of my worth as an artist in
money and skill instead of in meaning, because creating
meaning meant showing my heart—and what if no one liked
what they saw?

MATURE
co/or PALE tte
/

Fear of rejection is so common because there is always someone or something to reject you: a person, an entire community, a job, a feeling, yourself. Wondering if you're normal (you are) is an eternal question, and only when you realize that there is no normal will you stop asking the world for permission to be who you are. You'll spend your entire life running away from rejection, continually changing who you are, and still never escape it—unless you stand still.

Opinions mean nothing; they may be beautiful or ugly, clever or foolish. Anyone can embrace or reject them.

HERMANN HESSE, Siddhartha

The trick to becoming who you really are is to let your fear guide you. Instead of hiding from rejection, hug it closely: Put your arms around it and see what it has to offer you. Sit in the darkness. Feel lost. Examine the abandonment you feel. Wander inside yourself with a curiosity and a desire to understand your own thought patterns. Exploring a feeling closely dissolves the hold it has over you—and resisting only ensures that it will linger.

Ask yourself:

What am I afraid of?

Not being accepted.

Why am I afraid of it?

I want to belong.

What will happen if I don't?

I will be alone.

SO WHAT IF YOU'RE ALONE?

Nothing.

Aren't you alone now?

Yes.

Does your heart hurt?

Sometimes.

AREN'T YOU STILL HERE?

Doesn't every ache serve as a reminder to learn and grow?

DON'T YOU HAVE THE CHANCE TO TAKE ANOTHER BREATH AND TURN THIS AROUND?

Yes. Yes. Yes.

When we peel back fear and see that there's nothing hiding behind it, we begin to understand it. Like a cut that gives way to healing, periods of discomfort shepherd us into moments of intense clarity—if we don't accept ourselves, who will? It feels overwhelming because it's an acceptance of immense respon-sibility—we are accountable for cultivating our own sense of belonging, not someone else. The community we are searching for has to be built inside each one of us. What value does acceptance have if it doesn't come from within?

HAD I NOT
MY WHOLE
I WOULD
HAVE
IN OTHER

CREATED
WORLD,
CERTAINLY
DIED
PEOPLE'S

ANAÏS NIN

I painted portraits for two years. I took commissions because the client dictated what I should make—everything from content and layout to color and size. I didn't have to make any decisions, which meant I wasn't responsible for my vision failing.

What I really wanted to paint was wildlife. Majestic lions—kings of the forest, their faces framed by regal, golden manes—and angry tigers stalking their prey. I wanted to paint hydrangeas bunched up like the knots in my heart, lonely petals falling over themselves, forgotten ivy tangled up in-between it all. I moved from the sureness of acrylic to watercolor because the fluidity of it felt the same way I did. I was changing. I didn't feel in control. I explored my own feelings through color. I used reds and oranges because I felt angry. When someone saw the reds in my painting, did they understand how I felt? Did they feel angry, too?

You were born with your own incredible source of light: turn it on and take a look around. The sense of belonging you are searching for in someone else is already here. Like a constellation lit brightly beneath a foggy night sky, it didn't stop shining just because you couldn't see it. Acceptance is inside you. It's been waiting for you to find it.

If we stop contouring ourselves into the people others think we should be and focus instead on learning more about who we are, life becomes a whole lot easier: all we have to do is be. You'll find that there are entire stories inside you waiting to be told, hundreds of seeds waiting to be planted so they can burst into blossom. Where there is curiosity and understanding, there is beauty in difference. Where there is self-awareness and surrender, there is no shame in blooming alone.

Feeling alone is part of the human condition. It's how our body alerts us of a disconnect between our minds and hearts. We feel alone when we are out of touch with ourselves, when we are relying too heavily on something outside of us to feel whole. Fear encourages us to expand. It asks us to show ourselves, to take our pain and use it to make something honest.

It took me years to understand that the authenticity of being an artist and a human being both depend on one and the same thing: developing the strength and courage to be honest. Until I learned how to look inside myself, every painting I made reflected someone else's face.

Being aware of when you feel fear can prevent you from losing your identity or exchanging it for one that feels less vulnerable. The next time something is funny, laugh loudly because it feels good to do so. Be honest when someone asks you how you are, even if the truth feels a little too heavy, a little too much. Understand that if someone feels uncomfortable holding your truth, it's because they harbor a disconnect within themselves. It isn't your responsibility to fight for the world's approval. It's only up to you to give yourself exactly as you are—expansive and wondrous, containing multitudes—sometimes bruised, but always beautiful.

Now I paint wildlife. My work is bright, heavy under the weight of all the color I use. The yellows run into my blues and there is green everywhere. Now I make work that is honest and true—and although it doesn't always feel as if the world approves of me, it sees me exactly the way I am.

10

VENTURING INTO THE UNKNOWN

Have you ever held your tongue when you had an answer because remaining quiet was safer than being in the spotlight? Have you ever avoided telling someone you loved them because being alone was more bearable than the possibility of your feelings being unrequited?

Under the guise of practicality, comfort keeps us where we are so that we don't accidentally venture into The Unknown: a place of complete mystery—and magic. The Unknown is one of the most beautiful places we can visit, but we usually try our best to never go.

Like a shape-shifter, it changes constantly.

You'll visit The Unknown thousands of times in your life, and each visit will surprise you with an unseen landscape, dotted with churning skies and colors. Like anything new, this is simultaneously frightening and alluring. It's scary to venture into The Unknown because there is the possibility of danger and disappointment, but remember that there is also the possibility of beauty and surprise.

Anything can happen.

The Unknown is full of possibility. It's easy to stay away from it because it's uncharted territory, but if you can manage to tiptoe close enough, you'll see that the greatest gift The Unknown can give you lies in the not knowing: in the ability to open your eyes and see something new for the first time. How marvelous it is to see the winding branches of a banyan tree bending before you. How wondrous it feels to see a wild animal—previously accessible only on the pages of a reference book—mere feet away. The Unknown offers complete freedom. It's a blank slate— your chance to begin all over again.

You can visit as often as you like.

We're used to avoiding The Unknown because it's where fear lives. It's easy to associate The Unknown with darkness, anxiety, and disappointment, but The Unknown is a place that changes according to your perspective. Learning to think of it as a place of new beginnings, blooming possibilities, and beautiful change will encourage you to visit it more.
With each visit, you'll begin seeing all of the beauty you'd previously missed.

The first time I saw fear, I didn't recognize it for what it was.
To me, it looked like excitement and possibility: a giant cherry blossom tree that sprawled across my entire front lawn, its dark, twisting branches reaching up toward the sun.
If I climbed it at night, I could've easily reached the moon.
I wanted to understand what could be done, and I was interested in discovering my own capabilities.

Although it probably occurred to me that I might fail, I didn't operate from a place of fear. I moved, always, from a place of possibility. I wanted to try. The persistent, tenacious eagerness to try is a piece of magic we lose as we get older. It becomes overshadowed by the fear of failure. It didn't matter that I didn't make it up to the top of the tree. I could try again tomorrow, the next day, and the day after that. After all, time is just a stretch of infinite possibility—and fear is the reminder that this possibility rests in The Unknown.

the
UNKNOWN   BIG CHANGE   MAGIC

FEAR   POSSIBILITY   NEW BEGINNINGS

11

WHAT DREAMS ARE HIDING BETWEEN YOUR FEARS?

THE ONLY THING STANDING BETWEEN YOU AND YOUR GREATEST WISH IS YOUR GREATEST FEAR.

FEAR of FAILURE

FEAR OF LOVING MY IMPERFECTIONS

FEAR of HEARTBREAK

FEAR of COMPLACENCY

FEAR OF REJECTION

Artists are often admired for their work because it is difficult: it requires them to be vulnerable. Writers pour their thoughts onto paper and wait for others to critique them. Dancers rise early and practice for hours, going home to nurse their bleeding feet and aching limbs. Painters work tirelessly for months on end, only to tear down their canvases and start all over. No one will ever say that making anything worthwhile is easy.

We respect artists for their daring and punish ourselves for our fears, not realizing often enough that we are all artists ourselves. Living is art. Taking chances is art. Being present for ourselves and others is art.

Sitting with a friend who weeps from anger, loving another freely, helping a stranger because you see their struggle: these are the small blocks that build a full life—the greatest artwork of all.

Each of us has the ability to craft our own lives, and all of the elements we need are in front of us. Do you have a heart that beats and lungs that reach for air? Do you have a mind that turns and a spirit that moves inside you like a song? Then consider yourself lucky—these are the greatest instruments in the universe: they give you the means to create something out of nothing. Do you have a dream or a wish or a desire? Good, then you're already on your way.

If the pull of fear is holding you back from cultivating your dream, spend more time listening.

THE PRECISE
THEN, IS TO ILLUMINATE

BLAZE ROADS THROUGH

So THAT WE WILL NOT,
LOSE SIGHT OF

WHICH IS, AFTER

THE WORLD A
DWELLING

ROLE OF the ARTIST,
THAT DARKNESS,

THAT VAST FOREST,

IN ALL OUR DOING,
ITS PURPOSE,

ALL, TO MAKE

MORE HUMAN
PLACE.

JAMES
BALDWIN

Ask yourself:

What am I worried about most?

AM I AFRAID of DISAPPOINTING
MYSELF or OTHERS?

AM I ATTACHING MY OWN
SELF-WORTH TO THE SUCCESS
OF THIS DREAM?

What will happen if I fail?

If you're waiting for inspiration to hand you a dream, you'll keep waiting forever. Dreams aren't beacons that appear before us and then run the other way, daring us to chase after their light—they're combinations of the ideas, meanings, and actions that we value most. If you don't know what your dream is yet, that's okay—it doesn't mean that it doesn't exist, just that you haven't yet learned to recognize it.

Ask yourself:

WHEN DO I FEEL THE MOST ALIVE?

What actions do I
admire most?

IF I DIDN'T NEED TO MAKE
MONEY, HOW WOULD I USE
TIME IN A MEANINGFUL WAY?

If I wasn't afraid of failing, what would I try to learn?

Recently, I decided to travel across the United States because I'd never traveled alone and I was scared to do it. I knew I'd have to sit with all of the things that made me afraid and observe them closely. What would my fear feel like when there was no one to distract me from it?

I told myself: *You're writing a book about fear. There is no better time to scare yourself. If not now, when?*

YOU MUST DO the thing YOU THINK YOU CANNOT DO.

ELEANOR ROOSEVELT

I was afraid of loneliness. I was afraid that I was running away from my real life to something make-believe. I was afraid of disappointment, that traveling alone wouldn't be the glorious adventure I'd imagined, that the unease I felt in New York would climb into my luggage and follow me to the ends of the world.

Still I went. I gave up my apartment, along with most of the things I owned. I packed a weekend bag with enough clothes to last a week, said good-bye to those I loved, and told Brooklyn I'd be back in six months—maybe. *I probably won't last a week alone,* my fear told me, already disappointed over my ineptitude and inability to stand on my own feet.

A month into my trip, I found myself in Miami, taking note of my solitude and wondering why it no longer scared me. My fear disappeared into the ether simply because I had approached it, revealing a dream I never thought I'd catch a glimpse of.

Each day felt new, a chance to see myself for who I really was. I found that I liked looking into the mirror and more often than not, I usually smiled at the person looking back at me. I felt content, regretful only that for decades, I had failed to see the wonderful person who had always kept me company: myself. Had I been this afraid of myself all along?

Shaping a life, like creating art, is a process. It takes time to peel back the fear that layers itself between your heart and head. I am the artist. You are the artist, too. What great dreams will you bring to life?

12

FEAR IS HERE TO HELP YOU:
Find Beauty in Vulnerability

The hardest part about truly experiencing our fear is that it makes us vulnerable. With fear comes exposure— the experience of feeling raw, stripped, and shivering. The brain is wired to prevent us from facing discomfort, which is why vulnerability feels instinctually wrong. Telling someone that you feel sad or hurt is difficult because it invites harm—it's an opportunity to be ridiculed or to feel ashamed. But it's also a chance to show someone a hidden part of you—a small gemstone inside you that they might also recognize within themselves. It's only in this moment that you can both shine.

Feeling threatened by your own vulnerability is a routine, just like brushing your teeth before bed or feeling anxious when meeting someone new. It's easy to think that brushing your teeth is a choice and anxiety an involuntary reaction, but both are habits that simply became second nature over time. We develop neural pathways based on these routines, and the more we do them, they become further embedded into different parts of our brains. But if we choose, the threat of vulnerability can be overcome, leaving only potential behind. We can build new neural pathways that see vulnerability as a source of strength, something to hold close and cradle, not perpetually avoid.

IF YOU WANT TO
GIVE ANYTHING
WORTHWHILE
OF YOURSELF, YOU
HAVE TO FEEL
completely

EXP OSED.

Charlotte Rampling

Recently, a stranger e-mailed me saying that she would be visiting Brooklyn from California, and did I have the time to meet?

I wasn't sure how to reply. I had the time, but I also had a lot of anxiety when it came to meeting new people. Would I be liked? Would I live up to this person's expectations? Did I have the energy to perform, to behave in the way I wanted others to perceive me? It was easy to say no: I had the demands of my job, the demands of client work, the demands of any social life that desperately needs to be watered. Mostly, though, I had a very dark shadow that followed me around like a ghost, reminding me that this was another opportunity for someone to reject me.

I said yes. We met for a coffee that turned into a lunch and then a walk around my neighborhood. We talked about art, life, our conversations with other people. We noticed the sky and the sun and the way things are never what they appear to be. The stranger was kind, generous, and grateful. Her energy was palpable, infectious. I felt as if I'd known her forever. We connected immediately, energies colliding and coloring and reshaping themselves into something new. We were comfortable in our vulnerability—two strangers from across the country recognizing themselves in someone else.

Beauty is in the tenderness. Incredible change and growth can happen in these exposed, vulnerable places. It's after everything explodes that a star is born.

13

I'M HERE NOW

Creating anything—a song, a poem, a conversation—is hard. There are no guidelines or templates to follow. It's impossible to proceed with confidence. As a small child, I knew this and embraced the challenge. I liked the way strength escaped me when I read a poem aloud for the first time. The words made me weak in the knees because I had put them together myself. I knew what they meant. The meaning climbed inside of me and ballooned, lifting me higher than any story I had ever read in a book.

As I got older, the idea of continuing to identify as an artist became intimidating. The value of my work was determined by whether others liked it. My success hung on whether I'd be paid for what I made. It wasn't enough to simply create anymore. I feared not knowing when to give up for good.

At seventeen, I slipped into someone else's life. If I really listened to my fear, I could've clearly assigned value to what moved my spirit: Writing. Painting. Pulling something from nothing. I wanted to feel the magic that happens only when you open yourself up for the world to see. Instead, I did what I thought I was supposed to do—graduated from college, took the first job I was offered, quieted my needs and fears. I was avoiding failure by staying one step ahead of it. Or so I thought.

Inevitably, though, I began painting. From the very first moments, I slipped into a meditation, a suspension between my actual life and some effervescent state where everything made sense. Creating work that connected me to myself and others was an awakening, and for the first time in a long time, I felt like myself. To the external world, my life hadn't changed all that much, but on the inside, I felt reborn. I had purpose.

Every day I woke up and went to work, coming home to my second job as an artist, putting countless hours into something without a name—a dream? A relationship with myself that I'd never tried to nurture before? Over and over again, I built them both.

My fear of failure grew. It had never really left me, but it had changed shape. It looked more complicated now that I had something to lose. When it towered over me, I looked at it closely. What was this fear and why did it stay with me?

My fear mocked me. Who was I to become an artist? I wasn't special. Over and over, my anxious mind played its favorite songs. There were so many artists in the world. The market was already saturated with talent far greater than my own. It wouldn't be possible for me to find success, too.

Often, the work felt pointless. A lot of times, I never thought it would take me anywhere. I simply continued because it felt meaningful—and in times of frustration and tiredness, this meaning and purpose made it easier to keep trying. Like anyone who walks without a path, I made a path by walking.

That was six years ago.

The Unknown loomed like a make-believe bridge in front of me, daring me to come across. For a long time, I kept stepping back, edging away from the darkness that led to who-knows-where. I had a lot of fears. I held on to them tightly. Some of them are with me still. But six weeks ago, I quit my day job.

Now I put one foot in front of the other, walking toward something that has no shape, staring straight ahead into who-knows-where. It looks like nothing, but I know that it is the face of everything I've ever wanted coming into focus right in front of me. It looks like the face of a friend who has always patiently tried to guide me, even when I pushed them away. It looks like fear, and for the very first time, we're walking side by side.

I'm sitting on a beach somewhere on the southern coast of
Florida, my skin sticky under layers of thick humidity.
I am alone. The air is warm, salty. When I breathe in, my lungs
fill with nostalgia for all of the lives I haven't lived yet, all of
the people I haven't let myself be.

Behind me lies a vast stretch of sand. It looks like twenty
football fields that were emptied and filled with ocean floor,
placed back-to-back to create an entire stadium of nothing—
or is it everything?

In front of me, there is only water. The waves look large, but when I wade out into them, they don't knock me over. I lie on my back and try to float. The salt supports me like two invisible hands under my shoulders and calves.

I FLOAT ON.

In the water, I feel deeply uncertain and incredibly alive. My past self would've said that this was impossible: that I couldn't be two seemingly contradictory things at once. The first catch is that just because something seems a certain way doesn't mean that it is. The second, of course, is that anything is possible.

My fear has always
known this truth,
and now:

I know it, too.

YOU ARE A
marvel.
YOU ARE
unique.

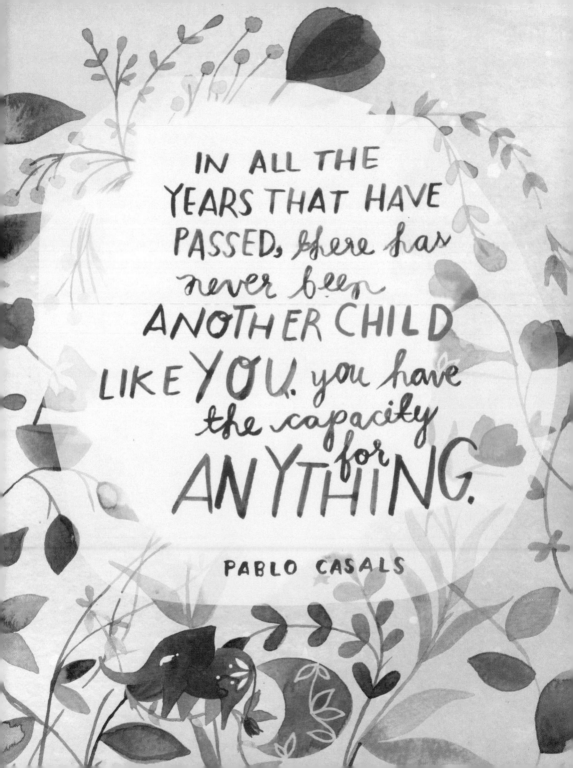

Epilogue

When fear came,
it came quietly and
something inside me knew

this was every chance I'd ever lost
coming back to me—
every wish I'd forgotten
slowly rising like stars,
brilliant constellations
pressed into
the sky.

When fear arrived,
it moved quickly but
something inside me knew

this was the darkness,
and yes this was also
the light.

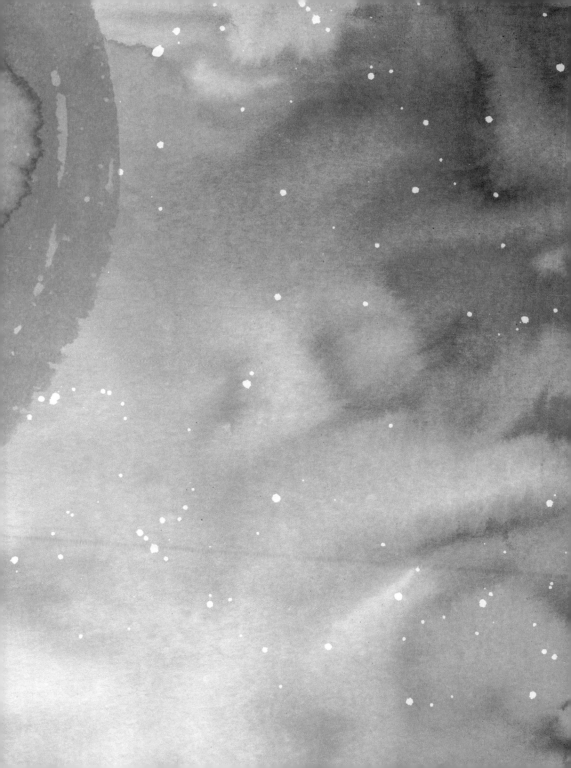

Notes and Bibliography

While writing *My Friend Fear*, I learned about psychology professor and researcher Robert Plutchik's psychoevolutionary theory of emotion. His books, *Emotion: Theory, Research, and Experience: Theories of Emotion*, Vol. 1. (New York: Academic Press, 1980); *Emotions and Life: Perspectives from Psychology, Biology, and Evolution* (Washington, DC: American Psychological Association, 2002); and *Circumplex Models of Personality and Emotions* (Washington, DC: American Psychological Association, 1997), written with Hope R. Conte, were invaluable in my understanding of the science of our emotions.

Additionally, quotations appear from the following publications:

Creative America by James Baldwin (New York: Ridge Press, Inc., 1962)

Discourses, Book III, by Epitectus (Cambridge, MA: Harvard University Press, 1928)

The Minpins by Roald Dahl (New York: Viking Juvenile, 1991)

Joys and Sorrows by Albert E. Kahn and Pablo Casals (New York: Simon & Schuster, 1974)

You Learn by Living by Eleanor Roosevelt (Louisville, KY: Westminster John Knox Press, 1960)

Death: The Final Stage of Growth by Elisabeth Kübler-Ross, 1975

A quotation also appears from the following film:

"Exposure" from *Charlotte Rampling: The Look* by Angelina Maccarone (film), 2011.

Acknowledgments

To Ojus and Jessica: you read, reread, and re-reread these pages not because I asked you to, but because you wanted to. For your kindness, critique, and encouragement, my heart knows no bounds. In fact, wherever you are, it's with you.

To Laurie: for believing in me and in my dreams, and guiding both. I'm so lucky to have you.

To Marian: for supporting and shaping these pages, and for always taking a chance on me.

To my parents, friends, and family: for your endless love. Without you, I wouldn't be who I am.

To you: for letting me be a part of your world, if only for a little while. We may be far apart, but we're both looking at the same stars.

About the author

Meera Lee Patel is a self-taught author and artist who creates work that inspires others to connect with themselves, each other, and the world around them. She likes sleeping and smiling and believes that all change comes from within.

Sometimes she is scared, but she still has dreams and is doing her best to leave no one dream untouched.

To see more of her work, please visit MEERALEE.COM.

To read her thoughts and see her smiles, please visit INSTAGRAM.COM/MERELYMEERALEE.

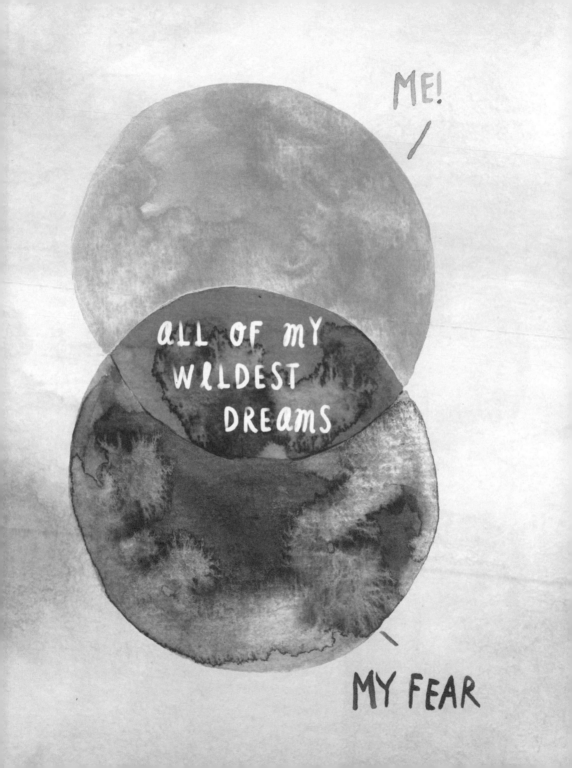

THE MOST BEAUTIFUL
PEOPLE WE HAVE KNOWN
ARE THOSE WHO HAVE
KNOWN DEFEAT,
KNOWN SUFFERING,
KNOWN STRUGGLE,
KNOWN LOSS, AND
HAVE FOUND THEIR WAY
OUT OF THE DEPTHS...

BEAUTIFUL PEOPLE DO NOT JUST HAPPEN.

ElISABEtH KÜBLER-ROSS

ALSO BY *Meera Lee Patel*

START WHERE YOU ARE

a JOURNAL *for* SELF-EXPLORATION

meera lee patel

WWW.MEERALEE.COM/BOOKS